THE CAVERNS OF OUR HEARTS

AN ADVENT RETREAT GUIDE ON ST. JOHN OF THE CROSS

FR. JOHN PIETROPAOLI, LC, STHL

Printed in the United States of America

Cover and interior design by Coronation Media

ISBN-13: 9798681325727

This booklet is a part of RCSpirituality's *Retreat Guide* service, which includes free online videos and audio tracks available at **RCSpirituality.org**.

INTRODUCTION

prò te
Domine pati, et contemni
B.P. Ioannis à Cruce Carmelitarum
Excalceatorum Primi Parentis ad-
uiuum Effigies

RETREAT OVERVIEW

What do we really want? We live in a world of competing desires. Every day we're bombarded by promises to make us truly happy. If you just buy this product, or read this book, or try out this dating app, or start this diet program, or exercise more, then you will be happy. If your relationship with your spouse or with your children or with your friends were better, then your heart would finally be full.

In and of themselves, these are not bad things. But will they fill our hearts? Is there a still deeper desire that nothing in this life can ever really fill?

In sixteenth-century Spain a Carmelite friar named Juan de Yepes wrestled with these very questions. History knows him as St. John of the Cross, and his considerations will guide our retreat.

In his work The Living Flame of Love, he offers a vivid metaphor to describe the human person's desire for God. Our hearts, he says, can be described as deep caverns of desire.

No matter how hard we try, nothing less than God will satisfy our hearts: As St. John of the Cross puts it, "They are as deep as the boundless goods of which they are capable since anything less than the infinite fails to fill them."

In some sense this is what the liturgical season of Advent is all about—and St. John of the Cross's Feast Day, December 14th, always occurs during Advent. It's a time when we wait and long for the coming of Christ—knowing that only he can truly fill our hearts.

And God, the great lover of our souls, wants to fill these caverns. In his writings, St. John of the Cross describes this process with unparalleled beauty and seeks to encourage his fellow travelers to cooperate with the Lord's work as he seeks to bring them to union with himself.

In today's retreat we'll explore that teaching in the following stages:

- In the first meditation we'll reflect on the foundation of St. John of the Cross's writing: God alone.
- In the second meditation we'll probe the importance of giving back even our deepest and holiest desires to the Lord.
- Finally, in the conference we'll tie these two meditations together as we ponder how we can continually give God permission.

Now let's turn to the Holy Spirit, asking him to fill the caverns of our hearts with the fire of divine love as we begin this retreat.

NOTES

FIRST MEDITATION

God Alone

INTRODUCTION

God does not deal in abstractions. The God of Abraham, Isaac, and Jacob is personal, and our own stories reveal his personal love for us. Moreover, our biography influences the way we relate with God, as life circumstances become part of our path to union with the Lord who loves us.

And the suffering St. John of the Cross endured forged in his soul the burning desire to seek the one love for which it's worth giving everything.

THE LIFE

He was born Juan de Yepes in Fontiveros, Spain, in 1542. His father, Gonzalo de Yepes, was the scion of a prosperous merchant family which disinherited him when he chose to marry an impoverished weaver named Catalina Alvarez. Gonzalo died shortly after Juan's birth, and Catalina was left penniless with three small children.

Gonzalo's family refused to help them, and one of Juan's brothers died soon afterwards, apparently from starvation. The image of the dark night, which would become an essential part of Catholic spirituality, began very early for Juan de Yepes.

As a teenager Juan volunteered in a local hospital, where he met a local businessman who paid for his education. With this preparation, at the age of twenty-one Juan joined the Carmelites, receiving first the name John of St. Matthias and later the name by which he is known today, John of the Cross.

He joined St. Teresa of Avila in her reform of the Carmelite order and became a superior in the male branch of the Discalced Carmelites. But reform is rarely popular, and in 1577 members of his own order kidnapped him and brought him to the Carmelite monastery in Toledo, Spain. At the time many religious orders had their own dungeons–luckily that tradition has been discontinued–and there John lay for nine months in a six- by ten-foot cell. His only intermission was the weekly flogging administered in the dining room in front of the entire community.

Yet in these apparently inauspicious circumstances, his relationship with the Lord grew. Abandoned by everything and everyone, God alone was infinitely enough. As John himself writes, "Faith and love will lead you along a path unknown to you, to the place where God is hidden." And God is hidden in the most unlikely places.

After his escape other members of the order continued to persecute him, but the caverns of his heart were filled with God and nothing could take that away. When a spiritual directee expressed indignation at the repeated injustices, St. John of the Cross replied:

> "Do not let what is happening to me, daughter, cause you any grief, for it does not cause me any... Men do not do these things, but God, who knows what is suitable and arranges things for our own good. Think nothing else but that God ordains all, and where there is no love, put love, and you will draw out love.
>
> —Letter to Mother Mary of the Incarnation
> **DISCALCED CARMELITE IN SEGOVIA, JULY 1591**

Throughout all of this, God created more and more space for himself in John's heart. God alone became his great desire, and he allowed the Lord to gradually fill the caverns of his heart with himself. At the end of his life, this process was so complete that St. John of the Cross's wish upon his deathbed was to die alone and forgotten by others. And his last words testify to his lifelong search for nothing other than God: "Into your hands, O Lord, I commend my spirit."

THE LESSON

What does all this mean for us? Sometimes we might think that we are called to imitate saints in the particulars of their lives, but this is not true. Each person has a unique vocation and a unique path to God, and it would be dangerous to model our lives after anyone but Jesus. For example, many of us would probably wonder if we could–or even should–request like St. John of the Cross, to die alone and forgotten. But that is not the point.

This is the point: The saints call us not necessarily to imitation, but to inspiration. They can inspire us to dream, and to permit God to bring those dreams to life. Even more importantly, they inspire us to allow God to bring about his dreams for our joy.

With that in mind, St. John of the Cross spurs us to some very important reflections. The caverns of our hearts are so vast that only God–the infinite One–can fill them. Yet most of us tend to try to fill them with someone or something else. We often approach other people or things with this more or less unconscious attitude: "I am going to offer you the chance of a lifetime: I am going to give you the opportunity to make me happy. I'm going to give you the chance to fill my heart."

TWO REEFS

If we're honest, though, sooner or later we realize that this is supremely unfair, not to mention impossible. No created being can ever completely fill our hearts. And with that realization we run up against two parallel reefs that threaten shipwreck.

The first reef is to keep trying to fill our emptiness with created things. Spouse. Children. Friends. Money. Power. Pleasure. The list goes on and on. But this is like trying to fill a bathtub without a plug. The more we try to pour in, the faster it seems to flow out.

The other reef is to try to repress our capacity to desire, reasoning that if we don't desire anything, we can never be disappointed. This was Buddha's approach to the meaning of life. But if we don't desire, we can't really love, and if we don't love we will not fully experience the life in abundance that Jesus came to bring. Along those same lines, it's no accident that John begins his poem on purification of the soul with these words: "One dark night, fired with love's urgent longings—ah, the sheer grace!"

St. John of the Cross helps us to steer between these two reefs. He encourages us to examine what our greatest desire actually is, and to relate that to God, again and again, so he can purify it. When we begin to understand the great desire for God which underlies all our other desires, God can start ordering our longings towards himself. Only when we long for him alone, and when every other love is taken up in the great love of God, will the caverns of our hearts begin to be filled.

As John teaches:

> "We must direct our hearts to God in joy and gladness that God is himself all this beauty and grace—eminently and infinitely so, above all creatures... If one does not turn one's joy to God in all things, it will always be false and illusory.
>
> —Ascent of Mount Carmel Book III, 21

St. John of the Cross was certainly radical, but all of us are called to radical holiness. Jesus's injunction to love him with all our heart, soul, mind, and strength–and to put nothing and no one ahead of him–holds true for every Christian.

In the next meditation we will ponder a scripture passage that illustrates St. John's point. But for the moment, let's bring all this to prayer, asking our Lord for light to see our own hearts as he sees them, and for strength to surrender them once more to him.

The following questions and quotations may help your prayer.

QUESTIONS FOR PERSONAL REFLECTION/GROUP DISCUSSION

1. How would I describe God's presence in my life right now?

2. What is my greatest desire?

3. How can I open that desire up to God and allow him to bring it into the safe place of his love?

QUOTATIONS TO HELP YOUR PRAYER

The soul that is attached to anything however much good there may be in it, will not arrive at the liberty of divine union. For whether it be a strong wire rope or a slender and delicate thread that holds the bird, it matters not, if it really holds it fast; for, until the cord be broken the bird cannot fly.

—Ascent of Mount Carmel, XI.4
ST. JOHN OF THE CROSS

"What more do you want, 0 soul! And what else do you search for outside, when within yourself you possess your riches, delights, satisfactions, fullness, and kingdom—your Beloved whom you desire and seek? Be joyful and gladdened in your interior recollection with him, for you have him so close to you. Desire him there, adore him there. Do not go in pursuit of him outside yourself. You will only become distracted and wearied thereby, and you shall not find him, nor enjoy him more securely, nor sooner, nor more intimately than by seeking him within you.

—Spiritual Canticle, I.8
ST. JOHN OF THE CROSS

For God alone my soul waits in silence;
from him comes my salvation.
He only is my rock and my salvation,
my fortress; I shall not be greatly moved.

How long will you set up upon a man
to shatter him, all of you,
like a leaning wall, a tottering fence?
They only plan to thrust him down from his eminence.
They take pleasure in falsehood.
They bless with their mouths,
but inwardly they curse.

For God alone my soul waits in silence,
for my hope is from him.
He only is my rock and my salvation,
my fortress, I shall not be shaken.
On God rests my deliverance and my honor;
my mighty rock, my refuge is God.
Trust in him at all times, O people;
pour out your heart before him;
God is a refuge for us.

Men of low estate are but a breath,
men of high estate are a delusion;
in the balances they go up;
they are together lighter than a breath.
Put no confidence in extortion,
set no vain hopes on robbery;
if riches increase, set not your heart on them.
Once God has spoken;
twice have I heard this:
that power belongs to God;
and that to thee, O Lord, belongs steadfast love.
For you do requite a man
according to his work.

—Psalm 62
RSV CATHOLIC EDITION

NOTES

SECOND MEDITATION

Lord, Whatever You Want

INTRODUCTION

> When aspirations born of love are unfulfilled in the way one imagined and understood them, they are fulfilled in another, far better way, and render more honor to God than was thought of in making the request.
>
> —Ascent of Mount Carmel, Book II, Chapter 19, Paragraph 13

These words of St. John of the Cross highlight one of the most profound and challenging aspects of our relationship with God. If the caverns of our hearts can only be filled by God, and if he wants to fill them, why do we have so many frustrated good desires? Why do the caverns often feel empty?

St. John, however, also hints at the answer when he goes on to assert that if God promises that our desire will be fulfilled, it will be, even though it may be done in a way different than what we had in mind.

Let's scan a scene from sacred Scripture that exemplifies this process.

> And Jesus went away from there and withdrew to the district of Tyre and Sidon. And behold, a Canaanite woman from that region came out and cried, "Have mercy on me, O Lord, Son of David; my daughter is severely possessed by a demon." But he did not answer her a word. And his disciples came and begged him, saying, "Send her away, for she is crying after us." He answered, "I was sent

only to the lost sheep of the house of Israel." But she came and knelt before him, saying, "Lord, help me." And he answered, "It is not fair to take the children's bread and throw it to the dogs." She said, "Yes, Lord, yet even the dogs eat the crumbs that fall from their masters' table." Then Jesus answered her, "O woman, great is your faith! Be it done for you as you desire. And her daughter was healed instantly.

—Matthew 15:21-28
RSV CATHOLIC EDITION

THE FIRST DESIRE

First of all, this woman was a Canaanite, that is, a pagan. She was outside the pale of Jewish culture and faith; therefore, her words to Jesus are bold in the extreme. Her desire, though, leads her to draw near. She is unknowingly responding to a process initiated by God, which St. John articulates in The Living Flame of Love:

> In the first place it should be known that if anyone is seeking God, the Beloved is seeking that person much more.
>
> —The Living Flame of Love, 3.29

What does she really want? It's interesting to note that the only direct request she makes is a plea for mercy. This is a very good start, as God's merciful love is the only thing that we sinners can rightfully claim. Then she goes on to say that her daughter is severely possessed by a demon, implying that she would like her to be healed.

This is a very natural and good desire for a mother to have. And yet there is something about the Greek wording that indicates something more. It says that she was repeatedly screaming these words, perhaps with some impatience. Again, that was only natural given the severity of the situation—but Christ wanted to give her something more. He wanted to give her the gift of faith in him, a faith that means giving him permission to act according to his plan.

Isaiah had already spelled it out centuries before:

> For my thoughts are not your thoughts, neither are your ways my ways, says the Lord. For as the heavens are higher than the earth, so are my ways higher than your ways and my thoughts than your thoughts.
>
> —Isaish 55:8-9
>
> **RSV CATHOLIC EDITION**

Jesus hears her veiled request, screamed repeatedly. He must have acknowledged and identified with her love and her desire for her daughter's healing in his own heart. And yet his response seems very strange indeed.

NOT A WORD

In fact, his only reaction is silence. Matthew tells us "he did not answer her a word." He did not say "yes;" he did not say "no." He simply didn't say anything at all.

Imagine what must have passed through this woman's mind. "I've heard that this Jesus of Nazareth is loving and compassionate towards all. I've heard that he cures the sick and casts out demons. He says: 'Come to me and I will give you rest.' My daughter is suffering, and I've come to him for help. Why does he repay me with silence?"

She would have grasped St. John's query in his Spiritual Canticle, when he asks the Lord "Why, since you wounded this heart, don't you heal it? And why, since you stole it from me, do you leave it so, and fail to carry off what you have stolen?"

The silence of God is a mystery that only faith can accept. By his silence Jesus asks her to give him permission to be who he is, and to act as he sees best—and to still trust in him when he falls silent.

In his silence, God tests our listening. He tests us in order to reveal what is in us—it's an instrument for us to become what he wants us to become. To draw us more deeply into his love, he will purify our spirit.

Her desire for her daughter's good is excellent; but unless it is taken up in a still greater love, the caverns of her heart will remain unfilled.

LORD, HELP ME

And the woman knows how to listen in the silence. She comes and kneels before Jesus. We can safely assume that she is no longer screaming. Instead she whispers, in a voice full of suffering, "Lord, help me." All her pain and all her faith shivered in those words. Any specific demand she might have had is gone—she simply begs him to help her as he sees best.

And Jesus responds, but his response seems even worse than his silence. He tells her that it is not right to take food from the children (the people of Israel) and give it to the dogs (the Gentiles). With his words, Jesus appears to reiterate that he will not help her. Why is the Lord of mercy so apparently heartless to this suffering woman?

Proverbs 25:2 reminds us that "It is the glory of God to conceal things, it is the glory of kings to seek them out." What does the Lord conceal in this ostensibly brutal reply?

God's great desire for us is that we come to long for him alone. Not "God and..." Not "God and my idea of how he should act." Not "God and my vision of what holiness should look like." Not "God and my family." Not "God and security for my future." Not "God and health." God alone, and in him we shall have all things besides.

And Jesus's words elicit a reaction from the woman that will echo until the end of time. "Yes, Lord, yet even the dogs eat the crumbs that fall from their masters' table." With this, her surrender to God is complete. She reminds Jesus of his goodness, and then leaves it at that. For her it is God alone.

AS YOU DESIRE

And Jesus exclaims "O woman, great is your faith! Let it be done for you as you desire." The creator of heaven and earth is deeply moved at this woman's faith.

She allowed him to ask her to give back to God, in some sense, her understanding of God himself. To give back even the greatest gifts that God gave. To give back everything and cling to God alone, in the nakedness of faith. Psalm 24 asks "Who can ascend the mountain of the Lord, and who can stand in his holy place? He whose hands are clean, who desires not what is vain..." He, in other words, who has learned to desire God alone.

What are we unwilling to give back to God? Holy desires, holy memories, holy hopes, holy ideas of who he is? When we surrender, it's not so much that we're giving up. It's that we're giving back. We're giving them back to God in order to be filled with him alone. Not "him and..." but "him alone."

This is now the Canaanite woman's great desire. May it also be ours.

INSTANTLY

The Gospel goes on to tell us that her daughter was healed instantly. When we trust to the depths of our heart in the Lord, he has space to act—and he acts instantly.

At times, after waiting and believing, our desires will seem to be fulfilled more or less as we hoped. Many times, they will not. But the Lord will always act, and the goal of all his action is to draw us into a deeper relationship with him, in faith, in hope, and in love.

And now the Canaanite woman could understand the words St. John of the Cross wrote in Spiritual Canticle:

> "When there is a union of love, the image of the Beloved is so sketched in the will and drawn so intimately and vividly, that it is true to say that

the Beloved lives in the lover and the lover in the Beloved.

—Stanza 12, Paragraph 7

As we bring all this to prayer, here are some questions and quotations that may help your conversation with God.

QUESTIONS FOR PERSONAL REFLECTION/GROUP DISCUSSION

1. What resonated most in my heart during this meditation? What could that mean for my relationship with God?

2. In my life, where is God trying to create space for himself alone in my heart? Was there anything that was in a certain sense "uncomfortable" in this meditation, and how can I bring that to the Lord?

3. What do I sense the Lord is asking me to surrender to his love? What would it look like for me to open my heart to the Lord and offer that up to him?

QUOTATIONS TO HELP YOUR PRAYER

"The heart is the dwelling-place where I am, where I live; according to the Semitic or Biblical expression, the heart is the place 'to which I withdraw.' The heart is our hidden center, beyond the grasp of our reason and of others; only the Spirit of God can fathom the human heart and know it fully. The heart is the place of decision, deeper than our psychic drives. It is the place of truth, where we choose life or death. It is the place of encounter, because as image of God we live in relation: it is the place of covenant.

—Catechism of the Catholic Church, number 2563

You enter God's apprenticeship only by persevering in prayers that are not answered... By its very essence, love only thirsts for love... The missed opportunity is the one that counts. Tenderness through prison walls: this is perhaps the greatest tenderness. Prayer is fruitful to the extent that God does not answer it. And sharp stones and thorns are what nourish love.

—Citadelle
ANTOINE DE SAINT-EXUPERY

Hear my prayer, O Lord;
let my cry come to you.
Do not hide your face from me
in the day of my distress.
Incline your ear to me;
answer me speedily in the day when I call.

For my days pass away like smoke,
and my bones burn like a furnace.
My heart is stricken and withered like grass...
For I eat ashes like bread,
and mingle tears with my drink,
because of your indignation and anger;
for you have lifted me up and thrown me aside.

My days are like an evening shadow;
I wither away like grass.

But you, O Lord, are enthroned forever;
your name endures to all generations.
You will rise up and have compassion on Zion,
for it is time to favor it; the appointed time has come…

For the Lord will build up Zion;
he will appear in his glory.
He will regard the prayer of the destitute,
and will not despise their prayer.

Let this be recorded for a generation to come,
so that a people yet unborn may praise the Lord:
that he looked down from his holy height,
from heaven the Lord looked at the earth,
to hear the groans of the prisoners,
to set free those who were doomed to die…

He has broken my strength in midcourse;
he has shortened my days.
"O my God," I say, "do not take me away at the midpoint of my life,
you whose years endure
throughout all generations."

Long ago you laid the foundation of the earth,
and the heavens are the work of your hands.
They will perish, but you endure;
they will all wear out like a garment.
You change them like clothing, and they pass away;
but you are the same, and your years have no end.
The children of your servants shall live secure;
their offspring shall be established in your presence.

—Psalm 102

RSV CATHOLIC EDITION

NOTES

CONFERENCE

Giving God Permission

INTRODUCTION

When St. John Paul II consecrated the future cardinal John O'Connor a bishop in 1979, Mother Teresa was ready. The newly minted bishop came down the aisle after Mass, bestowing his bishop's blessing on the assembled faithful. He noticed Mother Teresa and proudly approached to bless her. But before he could raise his hand, she grasped it in both of hers, looked up into his eyes, and said "Give God permission." O'Connor never forgot those words.

It's simple—not easy, but simple. God asks us to give him permission. Again and again and again, every day of our lives, he asks us to give him permission. St. John of the Cross puts it like this:

> When evening comes, you will be examined in love. Learn to love as God desires to be loved and abandon your own ways of acting.
>
> —Sayings of Light and Love, Number 60

Give God permission. In this retreat we've pondered the caverns of our hearts, which only God can fill. We've prayed about giving even our holiest desires and loves back to God. And in this conference, we will try to tie it all together as we discuss six ways to give God permission.

ACCEPTING GOD'S WILL

The first way we can give God permission is by accepting his will. At times we may have a vague fear of the words "God's will." Even as Catholics, we might think of God's will as a distant force that appears only in order to ask us to suffer something. But God's will is his love for us, and his love is his will for us.

This means that whatever God directly wills or permits in our lives is embraced by his love and is meant to lead to a deeper relationship with him. The French Jesuit Father Jean-Pierre de Caussade puts it well in his book Abandonment to Divine Providence:

> "The realization that God is active in all that happens at every moment is the deepest knowledge in this life of the things of God.

It's not always easy to believe that. But it's in line with St. Augustine's words;

> "Nothing happens that the Almighty does not will should happen, either by permitting it or by doing it himself.
>
> —Handbook on Faith, Hope, and Love, Number 24

We must not try to limit God's power. We say every Sunday "I believe in one God, the Father almighty." If he's almighty, then nothing is beyond the power of his loving care. "God is so good," St. Augustine writes,

> "that in his hand even evil brings about good. He would never have permitted evil to occur if he had not, thanks to his perfect goodness, been able to use it.
>
> —Unfinished Work in Answer to Julian, Book 5, Number 50

St. Therese of Lisieux, a spiritual daughter of St. John of the Cross, puts it another way in Story of a Soul: "It's whatever Jesus does that pleases me." Eventually she is even able to say, "I can no longer ask for anything with fervor except the accomplishment of God's will in my soul."

If we refuse to accept God's loving will for us in everything that may happen, we fall into the trap St. John of the Cross describes:

> Some souls, instead of abandoning themselves to God and cooperating with him, hamper him by their imprudent activity or their resistance. They resemble children who kick and cry and struggle to walk by themselves when their mothers want to carry them.
>
> —Ascent of Mount Carmel, Prologue, Paragraph 3

Instead let's ask for the grace to follow St. John's advice:

> Take no notice of who is with you or against you and try always to please God. Ask him that his will be done in you. Love him intensely, as he deserves to be loved.
>
> —Sayings of Light and Love, Number 155

This is a first way to give God permission—accepting his will.

BEING AVAILABLE TO GOD

Our obedience to God's will bears fruit in availability to God. Normally he doesn't ask us for dramatic things, but that doesn't make them any less difficult. What matters is that we give God what he hopes for, not what we feel ready to give him. St. John of the Cross asks "What does it profit you to give God one thing if he asks of you another? Consider what God wants, and then do it. You will as a result satisfy your heart…"

God may ask us to be available to listen to someone we don't want to listen to. He may ask us to forgive someone we really don't want to forgive. He may ask us to share his own suffering by some illness or confusion or loss. He may ask us to be like Mary, suffering at the foot of someone else's cross, only able to offer our prayers, our presence, and our love. He may ask us for something we never expected.

Think, for example, of the Book of Samuel. The childless Hannah begged God for a child, and eventually Samuel was born. In her joy, Hannah realized that God was asking for something more. He asked her to give her son back to him, so that Samuel could serve the Lord as a prophet. And Hannah did.

I can't imagine how difficult that must have been for her. Yet she did it. She listened to God's voice and brought the young boy Samuel to the temple to give him to the Lord. And it's beautiful to see how her availability to God was passed on to her son. A little bit later in the book of Samuel, he's asleep in the temple, and the Lord calls him. Once he understands that it's the Lord, he answers "Speak, Lord, for your servant is listening." He was imitating his mother's obedience.

Our availability to God will also be a blessing to others. When we make ourselves available to God, he will work wonders though us. We may see some of them. Most, however, we will see only in heaven. But sooner or later we will see them.

This is a second way we can give God permission—being available to him.

PRACTICING GRATITUDE

A grateful heart is a joyful heart. Remember Christ's words of gratitude to the Father in John 17:24: "Father, they are your gift to me." Jesus knows that we're not perfect. He knows that we're not always going to think and act from a place of love. But he still sees us as a gift. He sees us with gratitude.

When we start to see others and the world around us as gifts instead of as obstacles or as competition, we give God permission to help us gradually share in his vision of all things.

So, let's take time to rejoice in the Lord's work in our souls. Let's take some time to rejoice in the Lord's work in the souls of others. Don't let a day go by without thanking God. Don't let a day go by without thanking your spouse, your family, those around you.

A grateful heart is a joyful heart. St. Paul writes in the first letter to the Thessalonians:

> Rejoice always, pray constantly, give thanks in all circumstances, for this is God's will for you in Christ Jesus.
>
> —1 Thessalonians 5:16-18

And this means that we'll be able to thank God in good times and in bad, even when we suffer at the hands of others. As St. John explains it:

> Do not excuse yourself or refuse to be corrected by all; listen to every reproof with a serene countenance; think that God utters it.
>
> —Sayings of Light and Love, Number 143

Gratitude is the third way we can give God permission.

RECEIVE THE SACRAMENTS

A fourth way to give God permission is to receive the sacraments. (Normally that means the two sacraments we can receive again and again: Eucharist and reconciliation.)

This is how all baptized Catholics are called to exercise a priestly role. The Catechism reminds us in number 1547 that all the baptized are called to bring the offering of their own lives to the Lord, especially in the Sacrifice of the Mass. They exercise their priesthood by the unfolding of baptismal grace—a life of faith, hope and charity, a life according to the spirit. "They likewise exercise that priesthood in receiving the sacraments."

In the sacraments, we are drawn into the mystery of his suffering, death, and resurrection. To quote the Catechism again:

> Christ's paschal mystery is a real event that occurred in our history, but it is unique: all other historical events happen once, and then...they are swallowed up in the past. The paschal mystery of Christ, by

> contrast, cannot remain only in the past... The event of the cross and Resurrection abides and draws everything towards life.
>
> —Catechism of the Catholic Church, number 1085

When we receive Christ in the sacraments of reconciliation and the Eucharist, we are allowing him to gradually become the King of our lives. We are also bringing the whole created world to him. The sacraments are never just a solitary, individual action. They really bring the kingdom of Christ into a new birth, in us and in the world.

So, a fourth way to give God permission is to receive the sacraments, especially reconciliation and the Eucharist. How often can I go to Mass? Confession? Adoration of the Blessed Sacrament? Saints are forged by the sacraments.

SILENCE

A fifth way to give God permission is silence. The caverns of our hearts are vast indeed, and when we discover their enormity we often panic and try to fill them with something other than God. Noise is one of the most dangerous substitutes, and it's everywhere.

St. John of the Cross reminds us of the importance of silence.

> "The Father spoke one Word, which was his Son, and this Word he speaks always in eternal silence, and in silence it must be heard by the soul.
>
> —Sayings of Light and Love, Number 100

What am I taking into my soul? How much time do I spend absorbing local gossip, celebrity gossip, or political gossip? How attached am I to the news? What effect does that have on my relationship with God? How much space do I create for God's love every day? St. John asserts in Ascent of Mount Carmel that it doesn't matter if a bird is tied down with a thread or with a chain—in either case, the bird can't do what it's created to do. It can't fly.

Therefore, St. John of the Cross writes that:

> It is great wisdom to know how to be silent and to look at neither the remarks, nor the deeds, nor the lives of others.
>
> —Sayings of Light and Love, Number 109

He adds:

> Be hostile to admitting into your soul things that of themselves have no spiritual substance, lest they make you lose your liking for… recollection.
>
> —Sayings of Light and Love, Number 91

CHOOSE PEACE

A sixth way to give God permission is to choose peace. At first it might sound strange, since everyone wants more peace. But we need to choose peace in order to receive peace.

Jesus did not come to make our lives easy. He did not come to fulfill our vision of how our lives should unfold. He came to give us himself. His heart. His body and blood. His divine life. His relationship with the Father. His Spirit dwelling within us. His mission to help others know him and love him and find meaning in him. If we believe that, we will have peace in any situation. St. Paul boldly asks in Romans 8:35 "What can separate us from the love of Christ?" And the fruit of his confidence shines in I Corinthians 14:33 when he states that "God is not a God of confusion, but of peace."

Even sins and failures should not take away this peace. As St. John of the Cross puts it, "Because the virtues you have in mind do not shine in your neighbor, do not think that your neighbor will not be precious in God's sight for reasons that you have not in mind" (Sayings of Light and Love, Number 62). And this also holds true in our own lives—loving surrender to God, not sinlessness, is what is most precious in his eyes.

CONCLUSION: LIVING AS A MISSIONARY

The fruit of giving God permission is living as missionaries. Interestingly, St. John of the Cross doesn't spend much ink on the Christian calling to live as a missionary—perhaps because he simply assumes it's the natural result of a life lived in union with God.

When we give God permission to gradually fill the caverns of our own hearts, we'll naturally desire to be God's instrument to fill other hearts too. Remember, what God does through us is always an outpouring of what he's doing in us.

In this retreat we've explored the caverns of our hearts with the help of St. John of the Cross. As we prepare for Christmas, we ready our hearts for the Christ child who came to fill those caverns with his love. May we all receive the grace to give God permission to love us every day of our lives, and, filled with that love, may we become its vessel for every person we meet.

PERSONAL QUESTIONNAIRE

1. What's on my heart as I conclude this retreat?
2. How can I bring that to the Lord's love?
3. In what ways has the Lord consoled me or "challenged" me?
4. How or where is he asking me to give him permission?
5. Are there any "action items" God has inspired in my heart? If so, what are they, and how can I put them into practice?

NOTES

FURTHER READING

The Collected Works of St. John of the Cross
translated by Kieran Kavanaugh, OCD
and Otilio Rodriguez, OCD

The Impact of God: Soundings from St. John of the Cross
by Iain Matthew, OCD

The Fire Within: St. Teresa of Avila, St. John of the Cross, and the Gospel on Prayer
by Thomas Dubay, SM

Into Your Hands, Father: Abandoning Ourselves to the God Who Loves Us
by Wilfrid Stinissen, OCD

EXPLORING MORE

Please visit our website, *RCSpirituality.org*, for more spiritual resources, and follow us on Facebook for regular updates: *facebook.com/RCSpirituality*.

If you would like to support and sponsor a Retreat Guide, please consider making a donation at RCSpirituality.org.

Retreat Guides are a service of Regnum Christi.
RegnumChristi.org

Produced by Coronation Media.
CoronationMedia.com

Developed & Self-published by RCSpirituality.
RCSpirituality.org

Made in the USA
Middletown, DE
16 November 2024